The Xenophobe's Guide to The Russians

Elizabeth Roberts

D0777431

RAVETTE PUBLISHING

Published by Ravette Publishing Limited
P.O. Box 296
Horsham
West Sussex RH13 8FH

Telephone: (01403) 711443
Fax: (01403) 711554

© Oval Projects 1994
All rights reserved, including the right
of reproduction in whole or in part
in any form.

First printed 1994
Revised 1997

Editor – Catriona Tulloch Scott
Series Editor – Anne Tauté

Cover – Jim Wire, Quantum
Printer – Cox & Wyman Ltd.
Production – Oval Projects Ltd.

Xenophobe's™ and
Xenophobe's Guides™
are Trademarks.

An Oval Project
for Ravette Publishing.

Elizabeth Roberts would like to thank all
her Russian friends for helping with this
book, particularly Sasha, Lena, Leonid,
Katya, Yura, Dasha, Zhenya, little Sasha,
big Sasha, Petr and Tino – and of course,
Misha and Borya without whom things
would not have turned out nearly so well.

Contents

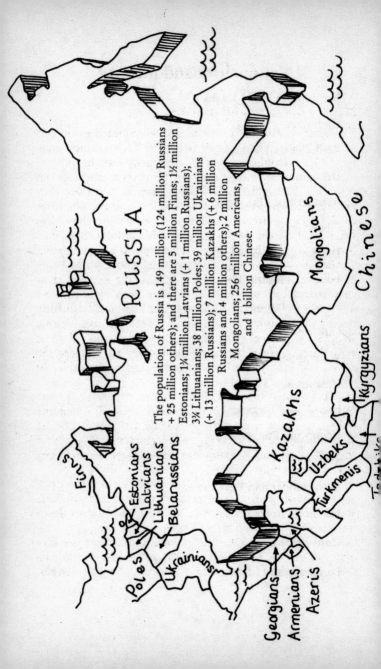

RUSSIA

The population of Russia is 149 million (124 million Russians + 25 million others); and there are 5 million Finns; 1½ million Estonians; 1½ million Latvians (+ 1 million Russians); 3¾ million Lithuanians; 38 million Poles; 39 million Ukrainians (+ 13 million Russians); 7 million Kazakhs (+ 6 million Russians and 4 million others); 2 million Mongolians; 256 million Americans, and 1 billion Chinese.

Finns

Estonians
Latvians
Lithuanians
Belarussians

Poles

Ukrainians

Georgians
Armenians
Azeris

Kazakhs

Uzbeks

Turkmens

Tadzhiks

Kyrgyzians

Mongolians

Chinese

Nationalism and Identity

How They See Themselves

The Russian attitude to themselves is summed up in one of their many pithy, earthy proverbs: "My country may be a smelly dungheap – but it's my smelly dungheap."

Although they despair of anything ever turning out right, the Russians firmly believe that, as a nation, they are destined to save the world. This is nothing whatever to do with the Revolution. This is something they have believed since the 16th-century monk, Filofei, described Moscow as 'the third Rome, and there will be no fourth'.

The Russians would like to be seen above all as being capable of running things smoothly while keeping their personal dignity intact. "The trouble with us is that we all have a serf mentality," Moscow intellectuals frequently muse. The playwright Chekhov talked of his lifelong struggle to 'squeeze the slave out of my soul'. This is sometimes misread by people in a hurry as 'squeeze the SLAV out of my soul' – impossible and undesirable, of course.

The Russians think of themselves as expansive, generous, open-minded, peace-loving and sincere. When the old Communist regime fell in August 1991 and the files were opened, they were genuinely amazed to discover that the Red Army really did have plans for invading Western Europe.

They will occasionally adopt a jocular, dismissive tone about themselves to test a stranger's attitude to them. One should not be taken in by this. They run themselves down but get angry if others criticise their shortcomings.

On the negative side, they recognise that they are lazy and not inclined to look ahead or foresee the consequences of their actions. Like Dickens' Mr. Micawber, there is a national inclination to rely on 'something turning up'. Their leaders were still boasting that not a single German jackboot would ever touch Russian soil when divisions of the German army were already hundreds of miles inside the Russian border, within striking distance of Minsk, Kiev and St. Petersburg.

How They See Others

The Russians claim to be passionately interested in the rest of the world. They secretly fear that to others they may seem somehow less than perfectly civilized.

They are relentlessly hospitable, for foreigners have to be humoured, above all in their extraordinary desire for such fads as time-keeping, sticking to agreements and doing things 'by the book'.

There has always been a tendency in Russia for foreigners to be treated differently from the natives. Foreign tourists have been allowed to queue-barge into museums ahead of a patient line of Russians who may have travelled just as far, or further, to be there. Many Russian cities have tourist hotels which were built only for the use of foreign visitors, and – notoriously – until the recent change of regime, Russians were not even allowed into the best hotels in Moscow or St. Petersburg unless a foreign friend met them at the door and escorted them in past the doorman.

Despite their apparently deferential treatment of them, deep down Russians do not think highly of other nationalities and their attitude to foreigners is both defensive and aggressive.

A telling anecdote concerns Tsar Alexander I who, while examining infinitely superior examples of English gun-making, fabrics, etc., observed to his General with a dismissive wave of the hand, "Of course, we have all this stuff at home."

Ordinary Russians travelling abroad adopt much the same attitude to the infinite variety of goods displayed in the delicatessens and boutiques of Paris and Berlin: "We don't need 200 different types of sausage." To a close friend, however, a Russian may admit: "We'll never have anything like this at home."

Despite the rather poor past record of the Germans (invading Russia, hanging men, women and children as 'examples' on their way in, and so on) the Russians regard the Germans with pity mixed with a grudging admiration. They rather respect them, and think of them as dependable and reliable. Fancy getting up every day and getting to work on the dot and working right through to 5 p.m. Order, application, thoroughness, finishing things – these are all qualities that Russians admire like other people might admire a contortionist in a circus. It's all quite extraordinary, but of course one wouldn't want to behave like that oneself. Germans settled widely in Russia in the 18th century, and formed the backbone of the shopkeeping class in St. Petersburg.

The Russians make fun of Americans behind their backs. They cannot understand how such a naïve, poorly-educated and stupid nation can be so rich. They regard the success of American industry as inexplicable and unjust.

The French are categorised as fickle, elusive, unreliable, strange and ludicrous. They are known as 'frog-eaters' (*lyagushedniki*). Traditionally, ruined French aristocrats were hired as tutors and governesses by good Russian families.

With the English, the Russians have a sentimental affinity. They refer slightly ironically to 'good old England'. It is known that the English make good shoes and umbrellas, and they like to imagine that London is still populated by men in top hats strolling about the smog-ridden streets which all Russians know about through their reading of Dickens and Thackeray.

Apart from their pubs, the Russians admire the English capacity for drink. In a story by Gorki, a group of Russian and English merchants agree to stage a drinking match on board a barge floating down the Volga. The last message received from the barge before everyone has drunk themselves insensible reads admiringly: 'The English ended up on Chartreuse'.

The Russians regard most of their neighbours with the patronising eye of empire. The Poles are thought to be sly and unreliable – even treacherous, capable of selling their own grandmother. The dislike is mutual. Polish women, on the other hand, are acknowledged to be beautiful.

The Armenians, Georgians and Azeris are thought to have depended on a firm colonial hand to keep them in order: "Now look what a mess they are making of their own affairs."

The Ukrainians and the Russians have a legendary mistrust of each other, rather like the French and the English. In one typical anecdote an old Ukrainian peasant is told: "The Russians have gone into space." "All of them?" he enquires hopefully.

There are many Russian jokes about the Chukchis, a small tribe who live in the furthest part of the Far East of Russia. Typical examples are:

A Chukchi enrols for a course on Russian literature at Moscow University. His professor asks: "Have you read Pushkin?" "No." "Have you read Gogol?" "No." "Tolstoy? Dostoievsky?" The Chukchi shakes his head. "Chukchi going to be writer, not reader."

Another Chukchi is driving his car erratically from side to side, careering all over the road. An old woman manages several times miraculously to avoid being run over, but when the Chukchi opens his car door he inadvertently knocks her down and kills her. The Chukchi looks round proudly, and says: "If anyone but a Chukchi hunter had been driving this car, that old woman would have got clean away."

Forewarned

There is no word in Russian for privacy. Russians not only have no concept of the joys of being left alone, they regularly demonstrate their sense of solidarity with the rest of mankind by going up to complete strangers, and for instance, ticking them off for not wearing a warm enough coat (if it's cold), or damaging a new bathing suit by sitting on the concrete edge of a public swimming pool instead of the grass (if it's summer). In church little old ladies come up and smack your hands if you are standing with them clasped absent-mindedly behind you during prayers for this is taken as a sign, like having your fingers crossed, that you are excluding yourself from the proceedings.

Perhaps the key symbol of Russia is the runaway *troika** at the end of Gogol's 19th-century novel *Dead Souls*:

'What Russian does not love fast driving? How could his soul, which is so eager to whirl round and round, to forget everything in a mad carousel, to exclaim sometimes "To hell with it all!" – how could his soul not love it? ... Is it not like that, that you too, Russia, are speeding along like a spirited troika that nothing can overtake? Russia, where are you flying to? Answer! She gives no answer. The bells fill the air with their wonderful tinkling; the air

---

*A carriage or, in this instance, sleigh, drawn by three horses abreast.

is torn asunder, it thunders and is transformed into wind; everything on earth is flying past, and, looking askance, other nations and states draw aside and make way for her.'

You have been warned.

Character

The Russians love to sit down for a nice long chat. Infrequently, but from time to time in their history, this has taken the form of a 'parliament'. Russian debates go on not just for years but for hundreds of years. They are still arguing about whether they should have anything to do with Western European culture and all the contamination of pure Russian hearts and souls that this entails.

Russians prize the quality of 'soul' (*dusha*) above all others. Providing someone or something has *dusha*, he, she or it is home and dry. Yeltsin has masses of *dusha*, Gorbachev had virtually none. People with *dusha* tend to drink too much, cry, fall in love, and fall into rivers off bridges on their way home from a night out with the boys. In Russian eyes this is a reassuring feature.

They have a tendency to 'open their soul' to complete strangers, telling everything about themselves even if the other person doesn't particularly want to know. The Russians are long-suffering but not exactly placid. They have a saying: 'It takes us a long time to saddle up, but once we are we up, we go like stink'.

What they admire is a spontaneous gesture – such as a young woman standing up in a restaurant to serenade a poet she recognises at a neighbouring table. They are generous to a fault. As you accept a share of their last crust of bread, an unworthy thought may cross your non-

10

Russian mind: 'Will he expect me to do the same for him one day?'

The Russians are extremely ingenious with bits of recalcitrant machinery. One distinguished old soldier who fought with both the US and the Red Army during World War II commented that of the two he felt safer with the Russians because when something broke it was mended there and then with whatever came to hand on the battlefield. There was no question of packing it in and going home until a spare part arrived from Seattle. Yes, the tanks were sometimes cobbled together with bits of string, and the planes flew on one engine. This quality is called in Russian '*nakhodchivost*' – the knack of finding solutions.

In Russian folk stories and fairy tales the hero Ivan Durachok triumphs because of his foolishness and simplicity. He is always asleep under a haystack when disaster befalls his cleverer and more ambitious brothers.

Russians are accomplished and habitual liars. This is something that has to be taken into account in business dealings and in affairs of the heart. They conceal the truth because they feel that it might be impolite to show the shabby reality. Thus for many years, gullible Western believers in the socialist paradise were led by the nose to view examples of 'Russian hospitals' (i.e. the one well-equipped hospital in the whole country used only by the Politburo), 'Russian schools' (the same story), 'Russian workers' flats' and so forth.

The habit of concealing the modest, not to say shameful, truth behind a bit of stage scenery was started by Catherine The Great's favourite general, Potemkin, who once lined the route of one of her royal progresses with 'villages' which were, in reality, mere painted façades.

Attitudes and Values

The Russian people's attitude to life is largely governed by the climate and the size of the country.

Those who are born in the vastness of the steppe, as soon as they are old enough, try to get a permit to live in a cramped, two-roomed flat in a blighted suburb of one of the major cities. One of the main reasons for this is their weather.

The Russian winter is known to military historians as 'General Winter' because of the decisive part played by temperatures of 30° below freezing in many an attempted invasion of Russia from Western Europe. The climate can be summed up briefly as: spring – wet: roads impassable from mud; summer – unbearably hot: roads reduced to dust tracks; autumn – wet: roads impassable from mud; winter – perishingly cold: roads impassable from snow.

Travelling across Russia's vast distances has induced a kind of fatalism about ever arriving. Russians always travel with something to eat and drink and something to sleep on – even if it's only in the Moscow metro.

Their fatalism can also take the form of a retreat into abstractions and grand theories, like bewailing the lot of old people in general while ignoring the plight of a particular old person in their own family.

Russians suffer from a feeling of a lack of control over their own lives. Everything is arbitrary, from whether there will be any meat or fish in the shops to whether buying and selling things at all is considered a capital crime. Daily difficulties and uncertainties have bred a certain endurance and fatalism into the Russian character.

The Russians value *posidelki*: the business of being in touch with people, such as sitting together in the kitchen drinking tea and talking about fundamental things well into the night. They also value *sobornost,* togetherness –

the feeling you get in a church on one of the big feast days, when you are squashed up against 500 other people.

Wealth and Success

Russian wealth has always been excessive. In the bad old Communist Party days, Brezhnev and his party chums used to enjoy limitless free airmiles courtesy of the Russian airforce. Children of the Party hierarchy would summon up a Tupolev to go partying in the Caucasus and, in one well-documented case, a plane was sent to Japan for a tea service.

Wealthy Russians buy private education for their children, *dachas* (small wooden weekend houses) or *cottedzhi* with every modern convenience, expensive fur coats for their wives and mistresses, a suit for every day of the week, mobile telephones and so on. The 'New Russians', newly-rich businessmen and bankers aged 25-35 years, waft along in a cloud of the finest eau-de-cologne, ostentatiously and expensively dressed in a signature burgundy-coloured jacket of cashmere or leather, dripping with gold (watches, chains, bracelets).

Russian jewellery traditionally has an unrestrained quality – enormous, often rough-hewn precious stones, diamonds, emeralds and rubies the size of pigeons' eggs can be seen displayed decorating ceremonial robes and ikons in every Russian museum.

This display of wealth is not particularly intended to impress. Snobbery is not a major part of the Russian character. Envy, and a bringing down of everyone to the same level, is considered more acceptable than allowing high-flyers their heads.

Russians believe in the limitless bounty of Mother Nature in general and Mother Russia in particular. 'Life is sweet, life is short. Tomorrow we may be stuck in the snow, so let's make the most of all our opportunities today.'

Religion

Religion is important to most Russians. Every self-respecting Russian grandmother makes sure her grandchildren are properly christened.

The Russian Orthodox church has never been wildly interested in social reform or 'good works' but giving to the poor was always considered praiseworthy until charitable activities of all kinds were made illegal during the Soviet period. Giving to good causes comes easily to most Russians – there is often a line of alms collectors (not by any means collecting only for themselves) outside a church or monastery and they are not chased away.

The Russian Orthodox church, with its dark, incense-filled interiors covered with ikons lit by the flickering light of candles and resounding to the chant of an unaccompanied choir, is the image of heaven on earth. It is not a place to sit and hear sermons about the evils of VAT on domestic heating.

To the Russians an ikon is not merely decorative, but a holy object in itself. Some of Russia's most venerated ikons are still believed to this day to be capable of performing miracles. In October 1993, the Patriarch of All the Russias, Aleksi II, had one of the most powerful images paraded round Red Square to seal President Yeltsin's victory over the rump parliament.

Behaviour

The Elderly

Khrushchev once joked that the Russian granny or *babushka* was the nappy-pin of the state, and indeed, many families have a little old lady living with them who may or may not be a relation.

Babushkas wear headscarves, and gossip, and go to church. In a mysterious way they are somehow made a whole size smaller than other Russians, but they make up for their diminutive height by being quite round. In character, they are sharp-tongued and opinionated. It is quite likely that when the President gets home at night, he gets ticked off by a devoted but critical little old *babushka* if his feet are wet.

Another group of old people used to be those eligible for the Politburo and the post of General Secretary of the Communist Party which ran the country. This special sub-set was formed because they all had information about each other and knew (in some cases, literally) where the skeletons were hidden. They are now either in jail or living quietly in rather nice flats and *dachas* around Moscow.

From time to time, on 1st May, for instance, or 7th November, a parade of elderly people appears on the streets carrying red flags and singing the songs of their youth in a nostalgic demonstration connected with the primitive 19th-century German cult or sect called Marxism.

The tradition of elderly rulers was held by many Russians to have been taken to extremes in the 1970s and '80s. In the days when Russia had a series of elderly and infirm leaders (Brezhnev, Andropov, Chernenko) a Chukchi rang the office of the Politburo, the powerful inner sanctum of the ruling Communist Party, to offer himself as the next General Secretary and Head of State. "Are you sick or something?" the politburo receptionist asked in astonishment. "Yes, yes," said the Chukchi enthusiastically. "I'm sick, and old, and I can hardly walk."

Old people continue to shuffle to work because there is no concept of honourable retirement, far less a generous state pension. For many of them, work provides one decent meal a day as well as company and somewhere warm to sit for eight hours. However, life expectancy has actually fallen for Russians in many parts of the country because of industrial pollution, radioactive fallout and other hazards, so the elderly may soon become a threatened species.

Children

On the whole, childhood has traditionally been a great, even the best, time in a Russian's life. In his autobiographical memoir, *Speak, Memory,* Vladimir Nabokov (author of *Lolita*) describes the idyll of growing up on the family estates in rural Russia before the First World War.

But in typically extreme Russian fashion, children are either doted upon and spoiled, or they are abandoned by their hopelessly drunken parents. Drugs and street violence are new and increasing threats to both categories.

National television programming is scheduled around the bed-time cartoon and Russians regard with horror the British middle-class practice of sending their children away to boarding school to be educated. Numerous private day schools have sprung up, but before that many Russian children were educated privately at home because their parents bought them tuition in such subjects as Classical Greek, Latin and French literature to compensate for the minimal timetabling allowed for these subjects in the state school system. Teachers' wages are hardly enough for them to survive, so they take two or three tutoring jobs in the evening to eke out a living. Peak demand nowadays is to help students pass their final school exams and university matriculation in foreign languages, physics, chemistry and maths.

Many Russian couples of late have only had one child, or, to put it another way, many Russians are themselves an only child. This is because living accommodation is scarce and cramped and the vast majority of Russian women have to go out to work and do all the housework.

Animals

The Russians love animals, particularly horses and dogs. One of their greatest contemporary conductors made special trips to London to get medicine for his French bulldog.

On the whole dogs are working animals rather than pets, so it is probably not a good idea to pat a Russian dog even when he is actually sitting on someone's lap, unless he is clearly a lap dog.

Inside every Russian there is concealed a hunter-gatherer, and given half a chance he will go off into the wilderness with his hunting dog, his trusty old gun and his fishing rod. Rural Russia still teems with game, and elks roam the outer suburbs of Moscow.

The Russians shoot bears and boars, and regrettably still use all sorts of animals as star turns in their famous circuses. A captive bear called Masha (short for Mary) is kept in a cage in the *kremlin* (fort) at Yaroslavl because the bear is the historic emblem of the town.

Eccentrics

The concept of eccentricity is hard to explain to a Russian. Examples from other cultures, such as the wealthy founder of Glyndebourne opera who always wore tennis shoes even with evening dress because he found them more comfortable, elicit a puzzled and worried stare.

On the one hand, Russians are in a sense eccentric en masse, being indifferent to the many rules and regulations which are supposed to govern their lives. On the other hand, after 1917, many of those who did not conform were killed – so that disposed of them.

Minorities

The Russians are quite politically incorrect as regards racial minorities and immigrants. In fact, it has to be admitted that they are – and have been since history began – fanatical xenophobes. In one of many testaments to this trait, Fred Burnaby, the 19th-century traveller to Russia, wrote in his *Ride to Khiva*: 'The Russians are as suspicious as Orientals'.

The word *pogrom* is the Russian word for an attack on Jews and comes from a root meaning 'threat'.

One of the first things that happened after the siege of parliament in October 1993 was that all 'Caucasians' (i.e. easily-identified swarthy Armenians, Georgians and Azeris) were stopped by Moscow police and their papers inspected. If they did not have a resident's permit, they were bundled on to planes back to Armenia, Georgia, or Azerbaijan.

People joke that when the authorities decided to issue passports to the Chukchis, they decided not to bother with individual photographs since to Russians all Chukchis look the same. However, one Chukchi came to complain. "What is the matter?' he was asked. "Don't you agree the picture looks like you?" "Yes, the picture looks like me, but that's not my T-shirt."

Manners and Etiquette

In their manners the Russians exhibit their usual failure to do anything by halves. They will apologise instantly if they interrupt you in mid-sentence, kiss your hand if you are a woman, help you find your way if you are lost in a city by actually going with you to your destination, how-ever far it takes them out of their way. Children are constantly being coached in good manners and ticked off if they do not come up to scratch.

Making a date with a Russian means exactly that. They never specify days of the week, such as "next Monday", or "Wednesday", only "the 13th", "the 4th" (of the month).

The general public used to queue almost as readily as the British used to – whether for oranges or to collect their coats from the cloakroom after a concert. Now jostling and pushing goes on in the street when getting on to buses, trams and the metro.

At table, the Russians help themselves without asking, which is a relief for Western Europeans and Americans who live in constant fear of inadvertently neglecting their neighbour. Russians consider it important to make regular and frequent toasts. No-one should even start drinking at table without making a polite toast to demonstrate that they are aware of their surroundings and want to share the pleasure.

No-ones finds it necessary to listen in silence while someone makes a speech at a formal social occasion. At an inaugural dinner and prize-giving of a major cultural award by a Western European company none of the Russian intelligentsia accepted their place settings, and chaos prevailed as literary and other luminaries roamed around the dining hall moving chairs and making nonsense of the carefully-organized seating plan.

Towards the end of the meal during the whole of which there took place an unending musical chairs as old friends greeted each other and exchanged gossip, the hapless chairman of the mighty Western conglomerate attempted to begin the formal part of the proceedings: the announcement of the winner. By now, even the top table had been deserted by most of the competitors and his remarks were drowned by a continuing hubbub of conversation. The Scandanavian co-sponsor then attempted to make himself heard, this time in broken Russian. In vain. Finally, the name of the winner was announced to the small group of diners immediately next to the microphone. The party going on in the rest of the room continued without anyone taking the slightest notice.

At the theatre or concert hall, it is now *de rigueur* to have changed into something smart. High-heeled shoes are taken in a bag to change into if it is snowy outside. Russian women are very chic and are currently basking in the new opportunities for displaying their awareness of fashion. The days of workers' dungarees are definitely over.

It is usual in a railway carriage to offer round anything you have brought with you to eat or drink; it is considered good form to be sociable and hospitable at all times, also generous. A visiting vicar was appalled when he was offered as a gift a precious old ikon of the patron saints of his host's church, one of the few pieces of genuinely old church furniture remaining since the church had been closed for 75 years. Luckily, the Russian incumbent was reminded by a parishioner standing nearby that the ikon (which was covered in gold leaf) would never get through the Customs.

Greetings

The Russians give each other bear hugs in public, men and women alike. Some observers noted as significant the marked absence of a bear hug for Gorbachev when he was met on his return to Moscow from his confinement in the Crimea during the August 1991 coup. However, it is claimed in his defence that he had banned the sentimental hugging and kissing that used to go on whenever one geriatric Eastern European leader met another and so the jury must remain out on that one.

When Russians greet each other they use the normal European repertoire: Good morning; Good day; Good evening or Greetings. They might follow that up with: "*Kak pozhyvaitse?*" (How's life?) Or "*Kak dela?*" (How are things/how's business?) To which the conventional reply is a shrug of the shoulders and the terse response: "*Normalno*" (O.K.).

The word *normalno* is very useful in Russian. It sums up what everyone there is yearning for: to live a normal life. Not straining every sinew to beat the Americans at their own game. Not leading the world in some mad competition to prove that 'our' system is better than 'yours'. A normal life is all the Russians want just now, thank you.

Not all Russians would go quite so far as the young soldier who was asked by a foreign journalist how the siege of parliament was going. As a burst of machine-gun fire made them both duck, he said with a shrug, "*Normalno*".

The Russians shake hands with strangers, but never across the threshold for that is considered very bad luck. When visiting someone's house or office you must either go all the way in, or wait until he has come all the way out, before greeting each other. Close friends kiss three times, for three is a lucky number. The Russians say 'God loves the Trinity' whenever things happen in threes.

Before leaving on a journey, Russians sit down quietly together for a few moments. This is (they say) to give their soul time to re-enter their body from wherever it is lounging about elsewhere in the house.

Names and Forms of Address

Like some other Europeans, Russians can choose between saying *ty* (thou) and *vy* (you) when talking to each other. Sometimes this is explained as being a simple choice between the intimate, informal '*ty*' and the more distant and formal '*vy*'. In fact, it is not as simple as that: sometimes perfectly happily married couples address each other as '*vy*', and seniors often address their juniors in, say, the office, or in the army, as '*ty*'.

Before moving on to *ty* terms with a social equal, it is customary to say 'Shall we go over to *ty*?' Of course, this merely pushes the problem back one degree, because the foreigner can be sure that the Russian will probably wait politely, if necessary for ever, before suggesting the move him or her self. In bed, it is different. There one moves to '*ty*' as a matter of course.

Once one has come to grips with '*ty*' and '*vy*' it is time to tackle names. Russians have three names: their *imya* (first name) e.g. Ivan; their '*otchestvo*' (father's first name) e.g. Ivanovich; then their '*familiya*' (surname) e.g. Ivanov. When you are introduced to someone, you are introduced by your *imya* and *otchestvo* thus: 'Ivan Ivanovich, may I introduce Stepan Kyrillovich?' But your host may continue to refer to you as 'Gospodin Ivanov' (Mr. Ivanov) to third parties.

To complicate matters, many Russian first names have a whole variety of affectionate diminutives, not all of them recognisable as connected with the original. Thus Ivan's mother may call him Vanka or Vanya, Nikolai can be Kolya or Kolenka, Alexander – Alik, Sasha, Shura or even Sanya, Dmitri – Mitka, Mitya. For girls, Mary or Maria is often made into Masha or Muma and Evgeniya becomes Zhenya (the same happens to boys called Evgeny, which is a bit of a problem). In many offices there is more than one Alexander, in which case the older one will be known as 'Big Sasha' and the younger 'Little Sasha'; anything rather than use their totally different surnames.

This trait is only too well known to the long-suffering readers of Russian novels, who constantly have to flip back to check whether Anatolyi 'Anatolievich Paskov' is the same as 'Uncle Tolya', 'my dear Tolenka', and so on. Illogical, but charming, it just takes a bit of getting used to.

Many Russians born during the Soviet period (1917-1991) have names made up of acronyms of heroes of the revolution, such as: Mels (Marx, Engels, Lenin, Stalin), Ninel (Lenin backwards – this is a girl's name), Dazdraperma (also for girls, short for 'Three cheers for the first of May'), Zikata (Zinoviev, Kamenev, Trotsky: this one fell out of favour in the 1930s when they all met a sticky end), Melor (Marx, Engels, Lenin, the October Revolution).

Obsessions

Talking, Drinking, and Secrecy are the great Russian obsessions.

The Russians talk incessantly. Unfortunately they find it extremely difficult to walk while talking. Going on a country walk with a Russian is actually an impossibility, because every time they launch into a new theory concerning the meaning of life or the relative merits of Arsenal over Spurs, they stop. This has led some scientific observers to conclude that the bit in a Russian's brain which controls his legs is – uniquely in the human species – connected to his tongue.

As for secrecy, a less polite word for it might be 'spying'. Throughout Russian history there has been a tendency to keep a systematic eye on foreigners and their technology. Most Russian hotels built during the Soviet period have a so-called 'service floor' where all the bugging equipment was housed and manned.

While it is now accepted that the Russians are enjoying a springtime of democracy unknown at any previous period in their history, and that foreigners and their capital are now welcomed, there persists a belief in some circles that the Russian information-gathering machine is hardly likely to have stopped dead in its tracks. On the contrary, its attentions may simply have been re-directed to Western technology.

Many Western firms now boast of the former KGB (Committee for State Security) colonels beavering away in their employ, easing the way through bureaucratic red tape and even providing useful bits of background material ons possible business partners.

Due to the purges and mass arrests of the Communist period, many people of otherwise blameless character got to know what the inside of a prison looked like and because so many people's flats were bugged by the KGB, a whole repertoire of silent gestures and coded messages have percolated into Russian life, the social equivalent of tapping Morse code on the plumbing pipes in prison.

The gesture to indicate silently that the person being talked about is a member of the KGB is pointing with two fingers to a set of notional military stripes along the shoulder. The one that indicates someone is an habitual drunk is a strange stabbing gesture with the index finger of one hand at the side of the neck.

A coded reminder that one's conversation is likely to be overheard is to point to an (if necessary imaginary) over-head chandelier. When Brezhnev was alive, he was referred to silently with both index fingers crooked to indicate eyebrows.

Drinking and Eating

"Drinking is the joy of Russians. We cannot live without that pleasure," stated Grand Prince Vladimir of Kiev as early as A.D. 988.

The Russians drink morning, noon and night. Many observers believe that Gorbachev's single greatest mistake, leading to his unpopularity among the Russian people and his eventual downfall, was caused by his unsuccessful campaign against the wholesale consumption of alcohol. It is rumoured that his own father was an alcoholic, which is not statistically unlikely.

Business deals are sealed with a colossal binge and Russians only feel really comfortable with a man if they have got extremely drunk together.

Modern Russian intellectuals and bureaucrats do not

drink themselves insensible on every occasion, but there is a severe alcoholism problem in the country. It is not unusual to see a man or (less usually) a woman slumped on the floor of the metro at any hour, or reeling frighteningly amid the traffic on one of the busy main roads. Bars on the street are mainly functional places with no chairs where men go to get drunk as fast and cheaply as possible.

Russian vodka comes in flavours such as pepper or lemon, as well as straight. It is drunk very, very cold from small glasses. For parties vodka bottles were traditionally encased in solid blocks of ice. The liquor should be so cold that it is almost viscous.

A very Russian accompaniment to vodka is *cheremsha,* pungent stalks of pickled wild garlic. The Russian way of eating caviar is very simple – no messing about with hard boiled eggs or chopped onion. Spread some nice cold butter on a piece of white bread, then add caviar and wash down with a swig of vodka.

Russian tea is drunk without milk and usually comes with a little side dish of *varenye.* This looks like jam, perhaps a little thicker and with more fruit, and is eaten with a teaspoon while sipping your tea. The Russians adore tea and claim that it tastes best if it has not crossed water until the boiling water hits it – i.e. it has come overland from the Caucasus, the Crimea, India or China.

Eating out in Russia can be a test of character. First of all, you need to gain admittance to the restaurant. This is not as elementary as you may think. An American oilman and some friends made their way into one of Russia's new pizza restaurants in Moscow at lunchtime and asked politely for a table. "We're shut," said the waiter, surrounded by the clearest indications that they were not. "And in any case, the chef's tired."

Russians have taken to the Western-type fast food outlets with such enthusiasm that they have to queue for up to 40 minutes for a hamburger. In St. Petersburg, a chain of restaurants sells something in a bun called a 'peterburger'. The Russian word for 'fast', *bystro,* which was exported to France by hungry Russian soldiery occupying Paris after the downfall of Napoleon, has been re-imported into Russia with the new French spelling 'bistro'.

The Russians are not one of nature's races of servants. Unlike say, the Italians, they do not find joy and pleasure in being of service. Russian literature is full of memorable servants who grumble whenever they are asked to do anything, steal from their masters and spend the day snoring on the sofa.

One theory is that Russian waiters must be engaged in some top secret project and some day Western scientists will discover what it is. Meanwhile, one thing is certain – they are all far too busy doing whatever else it is they do to pay any but the most perfunctory attention, or to spare anything but the minimum of their kitchen supplies to restaurant guests.

Some Russian restaurants, of course, are simply a place where the 'mafia' (underworld criminals) can sit in the warmth and keep their ammunition dry. Customers are not welcome at these places either.

Contrary to rumours, Russian food is delicious.

Breakfast is a big meal. It can include cottage cheese, pancakes (*blinchiki* or *syrniki* which are made with cottage cheese), jam, sliced cheese, cold ham, fried eggs, omelette or *kasha* (hot porridge usually made with buckwheat or semolina, milk and sugar, and eaten with lots of butter), sweet buns and ordinary bread, coffee, tea and juice. There is a great variety of Russian soured milk products, such as *kefir* (drinking consistency), *smetana* (sour cream), and most delicious of all, *ryazhenka* (soured milk baked in the oven to a golden brown colour.)

Most households stock up from spring to autumn with homemade pickles, preserves and jams from fruit and vegetables collected wild or grown in the countryside such as mushrooms, tomatoes, apples, blueberries, blackberries, raspberries, crab apples, cranberries and rhubarb.

Lunch tends to be at about 2 o'clock, if at all. The concept of fast food, cafés and restaurants is catching on, but not fast enough to find somewhere to eat at midday on every street corner as in Paris or New York, so it is vital to stoke up at breakfast time.

Dinner can begin at around 6.30 p.m. At either lunch or dinner the traveller should beware of overdosing on the first course (*zakuski*), with its tempting array of smoked fish, caviar, meat, salad, pickled mushrooms, cucumbers and so on – all washed down with vodka. Next comes the soup, usually clear, made with vegetables, and maybe a piece of meat floating in it or dumplings. Then comes the main course, meat or fish, with potatoes or rice.

Dessert is perfunctory, either ice-cream or compote (stewed fruit). Tea, rather than coffee, follows the meal.

The Russians have a very sweet tooth and serve delicious chocolates and biscuits with tea mid-morning and in the afternoon. From one small Scottish firm alone they import four million chocolate bars a month.

Leisure and Pleasure

For most Russians, the ideal way of spending the day is to collect as many people and as much food and drink as possible and spend the day enjoying them.

Having a patch of ground to grow vegetables is

increasingly popular and fashionable, as food in the markets becomes more expensive. Sometimes these small patches sprout mini-*dachas*, little wooden sheds just big enough to keep tools and seeds in, and even for the occasional one-person overnight stop. One step up from this is the *dacha* proper. Every Friday evening, families set off from the centre of Russian cities in small, ancient and overloaded cars bursting with Mum, Dad, little Petya, cousin Varya and her husband Kyrill, the dog, and enough food and drink for the next two days.

The Russians do not have flower gardens, they are content to be surrounded by birches and fir trees. In the autumn, many go out into the woods with a basket and a stick, mushroom-hunting. In winter, a masochistically energetic pleasure is to break the ice and swim in freezing cold water: this is called being a 'walrus'.

Sex

For over 70 years, Russians pretended in public that sex did not exist. But despite Khrushchev's witty claim that there were no professional prostitutes in Russia, only 'talented amateurs', there has always been a thriving sex industry.

Russian prostitutes exercise a bewildering and (to the lucky customer) charming right to charge less to men they find personally attractive. A good-looking young American businessman was approached in an expensive hotel by a Japanese businessman who wanted to share his pain and anger at being charged $300 a go with the establishment's call girls, whereas to his certain knowledge the same girls only charged Americans $100.

The same businessman was astonished at the sexual licence displayed by the wives and girlfriends of his

Russian colleagues. They were constantly coming up to him and inviting him to bed, adding reassuringly: "My husband (or boyfriend) says he doesn't mind".

But away from the free-wheeling circles of the new businessmen and the old 'mafia', a more puritanical note is struck. It is said that couples used to be advised by their priest to cover the faces of the family ikons in the bedchamber before making love.

The course of young love in Russia cannot run smooth because of the dreadful scarcity of places to perform. Secluded corners of stairwells, especially beside radiators, have been favoured, as have office desks after business hours.

Since *glasnost* was announced, newspapers and magazines have been increasingly obsessed with all aspects of sex, and Russian men have been taken aback by recent articles that claim they show less than total command of technique. The debate has even penetrated to the pages of the professional booksellers' journal, *Knizhnoye Obozrenie*, which published a 60-point sex questionnaire.

Sense of Humour

The Russians have a great sense of humour. They particularly relish the funny way in which life in reality differs from life in theory.

Some of the greatest classics of Russian literature are comedies – such as Gogol's play *The Government Inspector,* in which a young con-man arrives in a provincial town and passes himself off as the much-feared inspector from the capital, with many painfully revealing comic results. This, together with Gogol's prose masterpiece *Dead*

Souls, is as useful as a management consultant's manual for preparing to wheel and deal in Russia. Venality and corruption reign amidst a cast of unforgettable and quintessentially Russian characters.

Another very Russian genre is the so-called 'laughter through tears' (*smekh skvoz' slyozy*). Chekhov is a masterly exponent of the art of revealing how tragedy and comedy co-exist in everyday life. He firmly described his plays as 'farces' and 'comedies' and in his comic monologue, *On the Evils of Tobacco,* a schoolmaster sets off on an anti-smoking address, but wanders off the point to share with his audience the ghastly details of his private life, including his unhappy marriage to a domineering harridan.

In the old (pre-1985 *glasnost*) days, the only outlet for political comment was via carefully camouflaged, indirect humour. The clowns in the circus used to be famous for this sort of forbidden comment. There were also many variations on formulaic jokes, such as Radio Armenia jokes. For example:

Question: How much will a bottle of vodka cost in Russia in the year 2020?
Radio Armenia Answer: 200 yuan (i.e. Chinese currency).

Nowadays, there are stand-up comedians on Russian television whose repertoire is a mixture of political satire and imitations of well-known former politicians which would have been unheard of in the past.

The Russian language lends itself to wordplay and puns. For example, the reviled author of the simpering words to the Soviet national anthem was known with relish to his critics as the *gimniuk* (hymn-writer) because the word sounds comically like *gavniuk* (shit-eater). In Soviet times the authorities were sometimes referred to in conversation as 'Sophia Vladimirovna' after S.V., the initials of the words Soviet power (*Sovietskaya vlast*) – the powers that be.

Even senior bureaucrats may indulge in a sort of surreal humour. The Russian Minister of Culture stopped one of his senior civil servants at an official reception, knowing the man to be expecting notice of a long-awaited promotion. "Have you got my letter yet?" he asked. "Not yet, Minister," the man replied. A mischievous smile passed across the Minister's lips. "Ah. Maybe I haven't written it yet," he said, clinking glasses and moving away.

Culture

Big music, big ballets, big books: Russian culture deals in big things – from Tchaikovsky's *Life of Man* symphony to Tolstoy's block-busting two-tome epic *War and Peace*.

A crash course in Russian culture would have to include: the operas *Boris Godunov* (Mussorgsky) and *Eugene Onegin* (Tchaikovsky), both with librettos taken from Pushkin; something by Nikolai Gogol, perhaps his play *The Government Inspector* or his novel *Dead Souls* (imperative for anyone planning to do business in the Russian sticks – it's all there – the local mafia, the lying and cheating and eagerness to please the visitor from the capital); Goncharov's *Oblomov* about the Russian who could not get out of bed in the mornings; Turgenev's *Huntsman's Sketches*, to evoke the beauty and heartbreak of life in the Russian countryside; Chekhov's short stories; and any music by Rachmaninov, whose 2nd Symphony managed to reduce to tears not just the audience but the fairly hard-boiled leader of the London Symphony Orchestra at the end of a particularly withers-wringing performance.

One of the worst insults you can hurl at a Russian is that he is *nekulturny* (uncultured). In the 1960s, people used to pack football stadiums to hear poetry being declaimed. Now, rock music fills the big venues instead.

Russian theatres and concert halls offer tasty white bread open-sandwiches of salami, smoked fish, black or red caviar, cheese, bars of chocolate, and to drink, fruit juice or champagne to keep your strength up.

Literature

Most Europeans are aware of the great 19th-century Russian novelists, Tolstoy, Turgenev and Dostoievsky. But to most Russians, Russian literature is embodied by Alexander Pushkin, poet, playwright and founder of modern Russian prose.

The great-grandson of an Abyssinian prince who was imported to decorate the court of Peter the Great, Pushkin turned the language of his nanny into an instrument fit for the expression of the most subtle and passionate thought and transformed it into its present miraculous combination of freedom and order.

Pushkin was a romantic without illusions, a passionate lover who met his death in a duel over his flighty wife.

All Russian children learn a lot of Pushkin by heart and the rhyming nonsense verses of the great Kornei Chukovsky – a kind of Russian Edward Lear. Lear's rhymes have been successfully translated into Russian, and most Russian children know the classic English children's books: *Winnie the Pooh, Peter Rabbit, Alice in Wonderland* and *Treasure Island*. Shakespeare is standard reading in schools, the most popular translation being by the author of *Dr. Zhivago*, Boris Pasternak (whose family name in Russian means 'parsnip').

Every generation also loves to shudder at the witches-and-goblins world of Russian fairytales. The worst character of all is Baba-Yaga, a fast-moving witch who looks like a house on three hen's legs and eats children; most beautiful is the Firebird whose shimmering golden tail is portrayed on the tiny enamelled wooden boxes called Palekh, after the 17th-century town where they originated.

Cinema

Russian films are long. Russia's revolutionary rulers soon realised the propaganda value of film, and encouraged film-makers like Eisenstein to pioneer the 'docudrama' genre, in which the facts of history were shamelessly falsified to make a good movie. Some of the most famous scenes from Soviet history are actually film stills, notably the one of the crowd running across the square in front of the Winter Palace to 'storm' it. In fact, the Winter palace by then was unguarded save by a group of three or four young naval cadets and was taken by an almost equally small number of professional thugs who simply walked in through the back door. Similar liberties were taken with the storyline of *The Battleship Potemkin*, another of Eisenstein's heavily pointed farragos.

Connoisseurs point to Andrei Tarkovsky as the genius of Russian film. His early masterpiece, *Andrei Rubliev*, is a drama set in medieval times, which tells the story of Russia's greatest ikon painter and the suffering of the Russian church from the depredations of the Mongol horde. Later, his films became more abstract and darker in mood, including the autobiographical *Mirror* and science fiction *Stalker* which reflected the profound depression suffered by Russian intellectuals towards the end of the Soviet period. Sadly, Tarkovsky died in self-imposed exile in Rome before the great events of 1989 in Eastern Europe and 1991 in Russia finally set his country free.

What is Sold Where

Shopping in Russia is an adventure, not a routine. In country shops, amongst the plastic potties, witches' broomsticks and baths stacked in the middle of the dusty wooden floor, you may find wonderful glass and china, washed up somehow as if from a shipwreck on a South Sea Island, or exquisite linen being sold for a song.

The word most commonly used during the Soviet period in connection with shopping was '*defitsit*' – shortage. People would carry with them a string bag known as an *avoska*, a 'just in case', because a shopper might suddenly see the first supply for months of batteries or bananas, and wish to buy not just one, or one bunch, but as many as he or she could reasonably carry away. Now one can buy anything from a kitten to a complete hi-fi system from one of the hundreds of 'kiosks' or '*larioks*' which line the streets near every metro station.

Many of these goods are imported by the new breed of merchant venturer known as '*chelnoks*' (shuttles), so called because they bustle out to Turkey, back to Russia, out to the Arab Emirates, back to Russia, out to South Korea, back to Russia and so on, seeking consumer goods to supply a market starved of luxuries for 80 years.

The New Russians' French and Italian designer label clothes are sometimes made no further west than Derebasovsky Street, the garment district of Odessa, and expensive electrical goods labelled 'Made in Taiwan' sometimes prove to come from a factory in Siberia. 90% of cars in Russia's Far East come from Japan and are right-hand drive. These regions threatened to secede from the Federation when a law was promoted in Moscow to make right-hand drive cars like these illegal.

Trading hours in Russia's new shopping facilities are long: little old ladies turn up as early as 5.30 a.m. to sell milk, bread and tinned goods and stay until after midnight.

Newspapers, books and flowers can be bought in the *perekhody* (interchange passages) in the Moscow metro. Bread and seasonal fruit from the warm south – melons, tomatoes and grapes – are often to be found for sale on make-shift counters made from upturned crates at the subway exits. You are expected to have your own bag with you, and you do not get change without much theatrical performance, much sighing and searching in vain, until you say, "O.K., just give me the balance in prunes."

In Moscow it is not unusual to see someone selling books to motorists stuck in a traffic jam.

As the free market takes hold, small independent Russian shops have sprung up. They sell an extraordinary and unpredictable mixture of wares: a rack of second-hand clothes in one corner and the latest Japanese equipment in another. Old-fashioned glass-topped counters may display chewing gum, antique silver ware and aspirins side by side and all priced by hand in black ink on cardboard dockets apparently made from torn-up cigarette packets.

If you wish to buy anything in the more traditionally-run Russian shops, the following rigmarole takes place. First, all items are displayed on racks behind the counter. If you like the look of something, you catch the attention of the one harassed assistant, rather as you would try to buy a drink during the interval of a West End hit musical. When you have succeeded in doing that, she will reach behind her and put the article on the counter for you to examine. The routine continues until you have found something you want (this palaver, unbelievably, also goes for books).

When you have given the goods the nod, the assistant will write out a little docket which you take and join the end of the queue for the cashier. There may be up to 20 people in this queue, especially if it is a food shop and all you came in for was some butter. Finally, you pay for your purchase, and go back with the receipt for the goods, look for the original assistant who by now will have gone off duty, wait while her relief looks under the counter for the item and then about an hour later emerge triumphantly with your 250g of butter/pair of tights/latest Mills and Boon.

Strong men have been known to weep if they get outside and their wife says, "Oh, you got unsalted, I wanted salted", or, "Those are the sort with the funny heel".

A new phenomenon is the office equipment warehouse. This is an Aladdin's cave the size of an aircraft hangar containing everything from pencils to matching sets of executive leather office furniture, the latest IBM computers and even original works of art. Unlike the neighbourhood stationery store in the West, these places are guarded by men in army fatigues carrying Kalashnikovs.

One of the delights of Russian life is that no-one can be regarded as an infallible guide for long on the up-to-date minutiae of everyday living. No sooner does some pundit say "You can pay for anything you want in packets of Marlboro cigarettes" than hey presto, the kiosks are all suddenly selling Marlboros at less than you would pay in the duty free at Schiphol.

Time after time it's back to the drawing board for the foreign know-all, and the first-time visitor can be as wise as the hoary old-timer.

Custom and Tradition

When Russians die and are awaiting burial, their corpse lies in an open coffin in church. An English actress on a guest visit to the Moscow Arts Theatre found that one of the actors had died the night before the performance in which she and he were to take part. His corpse lay in state at the theatre during the morning, to enable his fellow-actors to take their solemn leave before it was removed for the family burial service. One by one, they went to kiss him goodbye on the dais, with his widow sitting beside him.

Forty days after a person has died, Russians celebrate the passing of their soul into paradise with a service and meal called '*pominki*'.

Easter is not a national holiday, but to the Russians it is the most important festival in the church calendar, because it marks the rising of Jesus from the dead. On Easter Eve there is a church service when everyone processes round the outside of the church with lighted candles. At midnight and during Easter Day and afterwards everyone greets each other with the words "*Khristos Voskrese*" (Christ Is Risen) in the same way others say 'Happy Christmas'. The reply is: "*Vo istinu voskres*" (He is risen indeed). When Brezhnev was increasingly incapacitated this story circulated: he was greeted in the tradition manner on Easter Day in the corridor of the Kremlin. Instead of the conventional reply, he grunted "Thank you". Minutes later, another functionary said to him politely, "*Khristos Voskrese*". "Yes, I know," replied Brehnev grumpily, "they've already told me."

At Eastertime, the Russians eat special food after it has been blessed in church: *paskha*, a sweet pudding made with eggs, sour milk and raisins in a tall rectangular wooden mould, the top patterned with the Orthodox cross and turned out like a blancmange, and *koulitch*, a sort of cake. Eggs – the symbol of the cycle of life – are coloured by being boiled in onion water for a traditional ochre, or with coloured paper to make them pink, blue, etc. Beautifully hand-decorated wooden eggs are widely sold in Russia at all times of the year.

The biggest national celebrations are held on New Year's Eve. Flats are decorated with Christmas trees, and Grandfather Frost (*Ded Moroz*, a white-bearded figure suspiciously like Father Christmas) with his assistant, the Snow Maiden, gives out presents to the children. Everyone has a party, and gathers round the television to see the Kremlin clock striking midnight, or they go to Red Square if in Moscow. It is the custom between adults to give a little gift – a decorated wooden box, perhaps, with the year marked inside. It has become smart to offer a gift representing the Chinese animal associated with the year ahead (a dog, a monkey, a rooster).

At a New Year party, don't raise your glass too soon as the clock strikes. For Russians, the magic moment comes with the twelfth 'bong'.

Name-days

The Russians celebrate their Name-day as well as their birthday. Every day on Russian television the list of saints whose day it is, is read out – Sergei, Anna, Agafiya, Vyacheslav, etc. On your name-day you get little presents such as chocolates or a bunch of flowers and you may have a party. The proper greeting is: "*S imeninami*" (Happy Name-day!).

In Russia a certain number of flowers is given, depending on whether it is a happy or sad occasion. It is customary to give an even number for a death, and an odd number on a joyful occasion. Flowers are given a great deal, for instance when welcoming people at an airport. When flowers are very expensive and the greeters are hard-pressed, the three tired carnations offered may well be on their third or even fourth time round, having been salvaged from a hotel bedroom as an honoured guest moves on.

About every two weeks there are other Days such as Rangers' Day, Marines' Day and so on. On these days, rangers and marines or whoever, gather and get extremely drunk and begin to fight amongst themselves and throw bottles at passers-by.

Russians like to celebrate the anniversaries of births and deaths of famous people. Not satisfied with marking the major milestones – the round centuries, or at least fifties – they have been known to throw themselves into 43rd anniversaries, or 167th as the case may be. Do not be fooled by anyone who tries to tell you that Russia is a 'young country'. It's just that their concept of time is different. They talk about the victory over the Tatars in 1380 as if it were yesterday, and mutter about 'another Time of Troubles' (*smutnoe vremya*) – which is as if an Englishman started talking about 'the Viking threat'.

It is an old-fashioned custom to 'wet' (*obmyt*), in other words to toast, a major new household purchase or even the award of a medal. In military circles, medals were dropped into a glass of vodka or champagne and the owner drank from the glass before removing the decoration and putting it on.

Health and Hygiene

The main care any sane Russian takes with his health is never to be admitted to a Russian hospital.

This is no reflection on the skill or dedication of Russian doctors, the majority of whom are women. It is because everything is in short supply, from bandages to painkillers. Russian doctors are poorly paid and operate under conditions of severe handicap. There are well-documented accounts of medical staff actually going out into the woods themselves to cut splints for their patients.

No Russian expects an anaesthetic at the dentist.

It is no exaggeration to say that Russian healthcare standards are at best fifty years behind those of Western Europe, let alone the United States or Australia. Not only are Russian doctors short of medicines, they do not have the equipment with which to diagnose what is wrong with you – blood testing, X-ray, and so on. As a result, ordinary doctors have had to develop an extremely high level of observation and diagnostic skills, long since ditched by their Western counterparts reared in the world of medical high technology.

The main physical complaints suffered by the Russians concern their stomachs, hearts and nerves. "Everyone is having a nervous breakdown," confided the wife of a Russian playwright. "I went to my doctor the other day because I wanted something for my nerves. Before I could even start telling her my troubles, she burst into tears and started telling me how awful her life was, and how she was afraid because her son is coming up to the age of military service. Her hand was shaking so much she couldn't give me the tranquillising shot I came for, so I left."

In Soviet times, many people were obliged to be unwell. "Ah, how often we were 'ill'," (*Skolko raz my 'boleli'*) remembers the soprano Galina Vishnevskaya who, with her globe-trotting cellist and conductor husband Mstislav Rostropovich, was at the beck and call of the country's political leaders. At the slightest hint of political trouble wherever they happened to be in the world, or if a local newspaper printed something deemed to be unfriendly, she and Slava were ordered to cancel their concerts on the grounds that they were 'ill'.

Another sort of illness, mental this time, used to afflict the country's free thinkers, who were confined wholesale to lunatic asylums and drugged up to the eyeballs. Soviet psychiatrists called it 'slow-developing schizophrenia' – a useful diagnosis for someone whose politics didn't fit.

There are now strict new laws protecting people from being committed against their will to mental institutions. As a result, there have been several unfortunate incidents where psychiatric cases have run amok and killed passers-by or even their psychiatrist.

It is rumoured that business recruitment consultants in Russia, when screening applicants for jobs, slip in a test for paranoia since a higher-than-expected proportion of the country's workforce seems to suffer from the conviction that someone, somewhere is still watching them.

Another Russian foible is their sturdy belief and reliance on folk medicine and faith healing. Charlatans thrive briefly and notoriously in the damp conditions of post-Soviet despondency. Odd characters appear on the nation's television screens, claiming to be able to cure viewers by thought transference. "When people cease to believe in something, they do not believe in nothing – they believe in anything", sighs a Russian philosopher.

The activities of these faith healers are usually brought to a halt by a flood of letters complaining not that there has been no cure, but rather that individuals have actually been made ill by action at a distance.

Another current confidence trick is the so-called

'bloodless operation' wherein a 'surgeon' and his assistant appear to remove someone's appendix by sleight of hand, leaving no scar. Quite prominent members of Russian society are taken in by this scam, and report the wonder to foreign friends in all seriousness.

Russian newspapers are always full of stories of mysterious cures, visitors from outer space, witches, wizards and so on, which evoke a tremendous response from the reading public. This is understandable given the failure of conventional medicine – and, indeed, science itself – to make life in Russia safe and comfortable.

Most medicine cabinets contain a liver and tummy remedy called *Nosh-pa*, their solution to that 'morning after feeling'. Many people, even relatively young ones in their thirties, carry heart drops with them. These *kapli* have been known to cause great excitement at Western customs entry points. The same Russians who carry the heart drops may also drink enormous quantities of stimulants, causing them to reach for their drops.

Caffeine is regularly removed from processed coffee for use in medicines which is why coffee bought in Russia often lacks the desired kick.

Russians being people of the woods originally, many of their folk remedies are based on trees: oak, lime and birch berries and blossoms are converted into creams and essences and infusions to be rubbed in or sipped. Other attested natural remedies include *Oblepikha* (Sea Buckthorn) whose bright yellow berries are made into a cream to heal radiation burns; *Chaga* (a sort of mushroom) for cancer and *Shipovnik* (wild rose), also for healing wounds.

Women battle with a lack of virtually every commodity: depilatory creams, razors, pads, tampons, contraceptives... Abortion is the most widespread method of birth control and there are over 10 million terminations a year.

The once-vaunted system of free polyclinics has long been a bit of a Potemkin village, i.e. an empty sham, and many Russians are cautiously exploring the new world of health insurance schemes. Even in the time since the official disappearance of the old USSR, many private hospitals and doctors have popped up. This has been possible because there was always a duplicate healthcare system known as the 'Fourth Department' which consisted of special Kremlin drug stores and other healthcare facilities for the Party faithful.

Russians have a charming, period addiction to spas and 'cures'. Until they lost their Caucasian empire to the south, people would regularly go to one of the numerous sanatoriums along the Black Sea coast of Georgia. They now take the waters in various mountain resorts in the northern Caucasus, which is still inside Russia, such as Pyatigorsk made famous by the romantic poet Lermontov who died there in a duel, Kislovodsk, or the eponymously-named Mineralnye Vody ('Mineral Waters') itself.

Many Russians have a bizarre desire to know their pulse rate two or three times a day, and for them a perfect present is a battery-operated digital blood-pressure taker.

Hygiene

Hygiene in private shared facilities is high. Each family hangs its own scrupulously clean lavatory seat on the wall of the shared W.C., but the state of public toilets, even in hotels or offices, can be indescribably filthy. Sometimes the loos are more like a hole in the ground, and very smelly. The mayor of St. Petersburg has introduced private public conveniences entered on payment of the same token used for the telephone and metro.

Despite the rough-hewn, provisional quality of the way

the hardware is joined to the wall, Russian plumbing works. On a visit with foreign businessmen to a provincial hotel, their Russian host worried all the way there whether there would be hot water for the shower. In the event, there was only hot water, so nearly boiling that the showers were unusable.

The Russians themselves wash in running water. Hence the mistaken canard about them being incapable of manufacturing plugs for the bath or basin. Bath towels are quite small and rough but very absorbent. The same cannot be said of their lavatory paper: small squares of shiny-surfaced paper, or torn-up copies of *Izvestiya*, if anything at all.

Their word for health is *zdorovye*. When someone has helped you with a task and you have thanked them, they may reply: "*Na zdorovye*", literally, "To your health" – or, in this case, "You're welcome".

Crime and Punishment

There is a saying in Russia: 'Nothing is permitted, but everything is possible'. This more or less sums up the Russians' attitude to rules and regulations of all kinds: they are there to be bent, broken, evaded or ignored. For example, it irritates Russians profoundly if their passenger fastens his seatbelt.

The fact is that there is virtually no reliably-interpreted system of law in Russia at present. Basically, the thing to remember with Russians is that everything is negotiable and can usually be resolved, if necessary by resorting to the time-honoured device of the offer of a bribe.

A bribe is not always needed. A young Scottish music

student discovered prior to her departure from Moscow recently that her passport had not been stamped by her hosts in Tver, a provincial city some three hours away. In Moscow she was warned that, without proof of her stay, she would not be allowed to leave.

Frantic with worry, and by now in tears, she was taken to a police station where her case was explained. "What were you doing in Tver?" the militiaman demanded. "I was learning some Russian repertoire – I am a singer" she stammered. His expression remained stony. "If you're a singer, then sing me something." She cleared her throat and gave him a full-throttle burst of Rachmaninov. As he listened, a dreamy look came into his eyes. He turned away, apparently troubled by a speck of dust in one eye, coughed and straightened his uniform before saying sternly "I'm afraid there is no question of us allowing a beautiful voice like that to leave the country." Then he smiled, fined her the equivalent of 50p and gave her back the arrest warrant as well as her passport as a souvenir.

The Police

Russian police on the whole are poorly paid, trained and equipped, and often physically unsuited to the job. Until very recently there was no system of selection – anyone mug enough could join the force. Foreign residents and Russian citizens alike have many tales to tell about the arbitrary 'motoring fines' levied by free-lancing policemen. Now, higher standards are being promised with better conditions of work and pay.

The Russians specialise in horrible axe murders and members of rival gangs often have machine-gun battles in the street.

Most people favour capital punishment. It is said that

when a Russian prisoner is sentenced to death and his appeal has been heard and turned down, he is moved to a special cell and allowed to wear special clothes and is given quite nice food. Then, one day, two prison officers appear at the cell door and invite him to follow them down the corridor. As he walks along, ignorant of his impending doom, a marksman takes aim from behind a half-open door and shoots him dead.

Prison conditions vary widely. Most are appalling, with pointlessly brutal warders. There are two 'luxury' prisons in Moscow, Lefortovo and Matrosskaya Tishina (literally: the Seaman's Rest). These are nicely furnished with good cuisine for prisoners such as the leaders of the unsuccessful coup of August 1991 and the equally unsuccessful leaders of Parliament who staged a sit-in and then an armed assault on the radio and television station and Moscow City Council offices in October 1993. There are said to be underground passages from the Kremlin to these two prisons, to make interrogation easier.

Systems

Most things in Russia, whether it be plumbing, telephones, post offices, trains, buses, trams, metros, rubbish collection, work – up to a point. It may be early, it may be late, it may divert three hundred miles to the west to pick up fuel or (in the case of plumbing) turn out to be a hole in the ground, but Russians get there in the end.

Attempts at reform in Russia often lead to the outcome remaining the same. For example, in the postal service letters used to be opened and thrown away if they contained unacceptable sentiments. Now they are just thrown away.

Peter Ustinov described how a retired German general maintained angrily: "We were defeated by Russian inefficiency! We had the best intelligence service available to any army at the time. I would even say that such quality was wasted on the Russians who talked on their radio telephones without any effort at disguising their intentions, without codes. We knew in advance that they would attack near Minsk with three divisions and air support. We knew the date, even the hour. And we were ready for them! But owing to Russian inefficiency those divisions never reached Minsk. Their trains ran out of fuel, and the local commander told them that he had no food for them and the best thing they could do was to attack the Germans and attempt to capture some supplies. As a consequence they attacked 200 kilometres away from where we were expecting them and by the time we reacted, it was too late."

Telephones

Telephone calls within Russian cities are free. This has led to a habit among city-dwellers of nattering on the phone all day long. You may have to try dialling a number again and again before you get through. On the other hand, an engaged signal or 'unobtainable' can mean 'you are about to get through'. At night, many Russians unplug the phone so as to get a bit of peace.

You cannot make an international call from an ordinary Russian telephone during office hours, and to make a call from a public telephone box you need low-denomination coins which have now gone out of ordinary circulation because they are useless for any other purpose.

In the old days when every call was bugged, a frequent visitor to Russia picked up the phone in Novosibirsk and clearly heard his own voice being played back to him from a previous conversation.

Banks

Russian banks are not regarded as safe places to keep money for the simple reason that they are often reluctant to give it back. Sometimes the government decides to freeze all banknotes above or below a certain value or foreign currency accounts.

In Russia, roubles are known as 'wooden' money. Many Russians got into the habit of changing half their salary every month from roubles into hard currency to protect its value, but to prevent this ruse the government stepped in and now controls the exchange rate.

Transport

Getting about in Russia takes patience and ingenuity.

For a start, a number of places have been renamed. Someone born in St. Petersburg at the turn of the century would have seen the city change name three times: to Petrograd (the 'burg' bit was thought unpatriotically German in the First World War), then Leningrad, and now back to St. Petersburg again.

Within cities, many streets have also been renamed, as well as metro stops. In Moscow, the famous Metro still works but regular users claim that trains are now fewer and further between and that standards of cleanliness are not so squeaky as before. Buses and trams keep to quixotic timetables.

Taxis have effectively disappeared from the streets of Moscow because they are hired for the whole day by businessmen. However, there are many so-called *levaki*

– private car-owners, often highly-qualified science grad-uates or redundant senior military personnel – cruising the streets looking for fares to augment their income.

Driving on Russian roads is like piloting a small boat on a choppy sea. Most Russian vehicles are old and much-loved, expelling acrid gusts of heavily-leaded petrol fumes as they trundle or bounce (according to size) along the highway. Russian roads have an air of only just hold-ing back Russia from under the tarmac, and in many places Russia has won through, causing potholes three or four feet across. Roadworks are unmarked.

A certain devil-may-care individualism in the national character governs the Russian style of driving. Close your eyes and try not to think too hard about how old the brake mechanism might be in the car you are travelling in so fast. When it is very cold, the windscreen freezes on the inside as well as the outside, so you may be kept busy if you are sitting in the front. Petrol must be paid for before you fill the tank – if you can find a station. More likely it's a 'flying petrol station' – a tanker lorry parked in a lay-by.

Passenger trains are popular, whether they are the local *elektrichka* or the long-distance Trans-Siberian railway. Russian trains run on wider-gauge track and are therefore wider inside than those in Western Europe. Groups of carriages on long distances are served by a stewardess whose main job is to stop the passengers opening the windows in summer and to keep a pot of tea permanently on the go. People on long journeys settle down to tell each other their life stories and packages of sausage, bread and bottles of vodka are brought out to make the atmosphere cosy and festive.

Flying in Russia has a piquant flavour of its own. Passengers on the state airline, Aeroflot, are not allowed to smoke on board and alcohol is not served. The seats are made in such a way that they tip all the way back to a horizontal position unless the person behind exerts an equally firm pressure to prevent them doing so.

A chronic shortage of fuel can lead to eccentric changes in routings. A customer boarding a plane for a three-hour flight in a northwesterly direction to Moscow from (say) Mineralnye Vody in the northern Caucasus might find himself landing after an hour in Grozny some way southeast to take on fuel. These re-fuelling stops are an opportunity for all the passengers to get out and smoke on the runway not too far from the plane. The mechanic carrying out the re-fuelling is also quite likely to have a lighted cigarette dangling out of his mouth.

Live animals are occasionally carried on board and fighting has been known to break out between passengers. Western oil men working in Siberia claim to have noticed Aeroflot pilots sharing a bottle of vodka on the way back to Moscow. Sometimes the pilot and co-pilot get off the plane, leaving their passengers sitting in their seats and disappear without explanation for up to seven hours. Sometimes the seats in the W.C. are sold to paying passengers who then resent having to move to accommodate the calls of nature of fellow passengers.

Winter

One thing the Russians really have got taped is winter. Russian houses are supremely warm and cosy. When you go into a Russian flat in winter, you take off your outside boots or shoes and put on a pair of *tapochki* – open-backed slippers, of which a supply in various sizes and states of ancient disrepair is kept by the front door.

All Russian coats have an intact hook at centre back of the collar. This is because you conventionally hang up your outside coat when you get indoors, whether it is a private house, restaurant, concert hall or university department. Every public building has a cloakroom by the front door manned by brigades of fierce elderly ladies or the occasional ex-army sergeant major. Woe betide you if your coat hook is broken or missing. They will look at you with a mixture of exasperation and pity. How could an otherwise respectable-looking and intelligent person have come to such a pass? No coat hook? Dear, oh dear. You'll be molesting small children in the street next, mark my words. The mutter, mutter, mutter, and shaking of the head goes on until even the most hardened non-possessor of a coat hook makes a mental note to get out a needle and thread the moment they get home.

Other features of the Russian triumph over winter include a range of crazy-looking machines with friendly nicknames such as 'the lobster' which beaver about in the streets clearing the regularly-falling snow. Any excuse (such as British Rail's 'wrong sort of snow' for failed points or cancelled trains) would be met with barely-concealed disbelief.

The Russians like a good hard winter with plenty of snow and frost so that they stay nicely frozen up from late October to March. In recent years the weather has let them down a bit, and thaws have been known in December, a phenomenon attributed variously to the use of atomic power stations or the mood of the Almighty.

Given a good hard frost, nothing could be more beautiful than motoring across the flat snowy wastes of Russia in winter, the firs and birches glistening white on either side. Or, to walk through quiet city streets in deep snow and experience *iney* – when the air appears to fill with sparkling tinsel as it freezes.

Education

There has been a complete revolution in Russian education as in so many other spheres of life in the past few years. School uniform has been reintroduced and each school is free to invent its own design.

There are many new private schools and universities. It used to be difficult to gain entry into institutes of higher education, but, once gained, educational qualifications counted for a great deal in terms of future salary and prospects. Members of the Russian intelligentsia are ferociously well-read and multi-lingual. But now someone can earn more in two days cleaning car windscreens than a university professor does in a month.

Almost everything in Russia used to depend on *blat* – whom you knew and what your connections were. Over many years of a non-monetary economy strange equivalencies evolved. A famous opera company had a special arrangement with a chicken farm outside St. Petersburg. The farm workers got tickets for the Kirov Opera and the singers got eggs. What could be more logical?

Conscription

Theoretically conscription into the Russian army exists. Every boy aged 18 could be called up to serve for 18 months (or 3 years in the marines), but there are certain exemptions for further education or, for instance, professional musical training. In any case an estimated one in three does not respond.

The Russian army, like British public schools, has a fearful reputation for bullying and violence, including male rape. It varies in quality from world-class excellence in some units (the *spetsnaz*, commandos) to laughably bad (those sent to keep the peace in former Yugoslavia, who dealt in aid packages on the black market and whose commander drove round in a white Mercedes bought with the proceeds).

The military is in the gradual process of converting itself into an all-professional outfit, and jobs are being sought for the 400,000 spare officers due to be demobbed under various troop reduction agreements. The Minister of Defence is said to be open to any suggestions.

Government and Bureaucracy

The Russians are used to being badly governed. They have been badly governed for nearly one thousand years. In their history, to date, the only alternative the Russians know to being badly governed is to have no government at all.

The sheer physical size of Russia and its many constituent ethnic minorities have combined to defeat most attempts at government. When the centre is weak, local governors' rule can become arbitrary. Thus the pendulum has tended to swing between authoritarian repression and 'chaos spiralling down to anarchy'.

One of Russia's reforming Tsarist Ministers, Count Witte, said: "The world should be surprised that we have any government in Russia, not that we have an imperfect government."

Bureaucracy

The amount of bureaucracy in everyday life is stunning. This is because it pays. When Russia was a one-party state, there used to be a joke that they couldn't afford democracy because the one party they had cost too much already.

Corruption was and is universal. Things have got worse. A party card was a passport to the good life, and was not open to any Tom, Dick or Dirty Harry. Now, anyone can play, and the stakes are high. Nothing can move without the right *bumazhka* or *spravka* (bit of official paper, chitty, bumph). There is a Russian saying: 'Without a chitty, you're a worm, But with a chit: a man.'

Taxes on some new enterprises are in excess of 100% which means, of course, that wherever possible the rules are evaded or bribes are offered to effect a shortcut through the jungle of red tape. The traditional solution for Western companies or individuals who wish to avoid direct collusion is to appoint a local agent who will do the necessary on their behalf. Bribes are usually offered in dollars.

The Russians have never had the right to free movement whether within their own country or abroad. You have to apply for permission to go and live in another city within Russia, and that permission is very often conditional upon being able to show that you have a job and a place to live there – a kind of Catch 22. This is one of the reasons that two or three generations of a family in Moscow squash together, all living in the one small flat. Adult children do not wish to move out even after they marry because then they might lose their right to live in Moscow itself.

Since 1992, each citizen has the right to possess a foreign passport, which for the first time in Russian history gives them the right to leave Russia any time they like. Sticklers have noticed with some surprise that the cover of many of these 'new' passports still bear the hammer and sickle emblem and title of the defunct Soviet Union. 'Waste not, want not' is a rule observed by bureaucrats the world over.

Business

For Russians the ideal job is summed up in the verb *sidet*, which means 'to sit'. By this they mean where one does as little as possible for as much money as possible. This includes coming in late, if at all, and leaving early.

Seventy years of Socialism on top of a natural inclination to take life easy has dealt a hammer blow to any notions of Russian get-up-and-go. A young Russian entrepreneur hired a middle-aged woman as a receptionist-cum-research assistant for an outpost of his very busy new computer bureau. The following day, at about noon, an enraged customer rang to complain that he had been waiting outside the office since 9 a.m. and no-one had appeared to open up. The young entrepreneur rushed over himself and dealt with the customer and later – much later – at 3 p.m., the new receptionist strolled in. "Lydia Ivanovna! What is the meaning of this?" her new employer cried. "I had a call from my old office to say they had some fresh fish in and so I went over there first," she explained, quite hurt by his exasperation.

An English transport specialist based in Russia remembers finding out when he began working there some years ago it could routinely take up to four months to clear goods from the port of arrival and up to a year to get them to their destination. If a problem arose, his staff would instinctively shove it under the carpet rather than tell. "Nobody wants to take responsibility. They never apologise and they lie without shame. Even when they are found out to be lying, they just shrug their shoulders." It has to be added that this Englishman is building a house for his family to settle in Russia.

"They want all the benefits without doing any of the work" says another foreign technician working in Russia. "It takes three of them do do a job which one man would

56

do in England or America. If there is a piece of equipment, one will drive it and another one will operate it while a third watches. Everyone wants to be paid in cash. No-one trusts the banks and there is no loan system. Everyone has his own scheme, and is competing to do his own deal."

"When I needed to buy a new truck for the business", the transport specialist recalls, "every single member of my staff came to me individually and told me he could get me a new truck for such-and-such a price, cheaper and cheaper. But the truck never materialised and in the end I told them all to sod off and bought one for the advertised price."

Yet when Russians do set their minds to it, they can swing into action fast and deliver on the nail. "If you get a Russian who is money-motivated, they can make anything happen", says an American oilman. This can sometimes be alarming, as one Western businessman discovered when he was enquiring about getting a consignment of timber out and his counterpart explained that delivery was no problem: when they needed transport a train would be stolen.

"Position, power and money are what count in this country. If a Russian feels he has a future with you, that will motivate him – they don't have any other security in their lives, no mortgage, no pension, nothing", explains a French resident of Moscow.

New Russians drive fast foreign cars recklessly ignoring all the traffic rules, are swaggering and self-confident, have beautiful girls hanging on their arm, expensive bathrooms and constantly travel abroad. Russian teenagers used to be sensitive and naïve. Now their one aim is to work for a 'joint venture' or a bank. They have absolutely no principles.

Numerous young Russians have taken to the free

market economy like ducks to water. Unfortunately, many 'wide boys' from the West have rushed in to fill the vacuum and there are shameful stories in many Moscow business circles of Western partners disappearing with the loot. Some observers liken present-day Russia to what the USA must have been like in the 1870s. A 'Wild West' mentality prevails, fortunes are being made and lives sometimes lost in the scramble. Conditions of business in Russia can be changed by the government overnight without notice – for instance, taxes on imports. It's heady stuff – if you can stand the pace.

The older Russians are 'plan' oriented and get quite upset if they have to make changes at short notice. They tend not to have back-up or contingency plans – no Plan B in case Plan A fails.

There is an oriental streak in Russian business practice. 'Scratch a Russian and find a Tatar', runs an old saying. They will hold endless getting-to-know-you meetings. Delegations will go back and forth. After a while the Western business person may think the whole thing is a waste of time. But once he is 'in', he can usually rely on his business partners.

As far as management skills go, very few Russians know how to keep accounts or draw up a business plan but they are learning fast. Business and marketing manuals are extremely popular and sell out as fast as the bookshops can stack the shelves.

Shares are now available for purchase on every street corner in practically every human activity, including esoteric investments such as the Economics Department of Moscow University.

The science of the 'bottom line' is in its infancy, as witness the story of the Russian who came home in the early hours after gambling all night and said "Darling! I've had an extraordinary run of luck! You know that coat

I bought for 100,000 roubles – I lost it for 150,000!"
Today the New Russian joke goes: Two new Russians
meet and one says "I bought a new tie in London for $70."
The other says: "You idiot! You could have got one in
Paris for more than $100."

Apart from the new business-oriented class, Russians
tend to take a laid-back attitude to getting things done.
The Russian countryside is littered with tractors and
other bits of expensive machinery which have just been
left out to die. Under the old Soviet system, everything
belonged to everyone and therefore, in practice, to no-
one. The concept of keeping to schedule, looking after
things properly and feeling a sense of personal responsibility for a project may never take root in quite the same
way as it has in Western Europe.

Most Russians, if asked what they hope to achieve in
business, will waffle about doing good for mankind
rather than homing in on the profit motive. The Russians
are uneasy about financial success. They assume (from
their own national experience and therefore possibly with
some justification) that great wealth has been come by
dishonestly or at the least at someone else's, and probably
their own, expense. "99% of our businessmen are thieves,
criminals and outlaws. People hate them," states one
Russian computer scientist.

Relations between staff in business offices tend to be
old-fashioned. Russians who go to work in the West are
sometimes disappointed at how little human contact is
made with colleagues outside working hours, including
walking along the road together to the bus stop or underground station. Russian work teams tend to develop a
family atmosphere, rallying round in times of domestic
crisis or tragedy. In one case where a young office worker
was murdered in his flat, his workmates took it upon
themselves to organize the formalities and the funeral.

Superiors address their juniors, drivers, etc., by affectionate diminutives which might be considered patronising or chauvinist between employees of either sex in the West. But there again, how many City of London bankers are used to finding their driver curled up asleep on the back seat of the office car which is perfectly standard practice in Russia. Working hours are very long and drivers need the odd nip of vodka to keep out the cold.

Government officials in Russia usually wear a suit. Formal wear is also worn in some 'new' business circles, such as commodity dealing and merchant banking. In most other offices and enterprises dress is casual, some emulating the Richard Branson style of patterned jumper. New Russians who have made their first million sometimes carry it with them in a suitcase, in which event they are also equipped with small armies of very serious-looking private bodyguards armed to the teeth with sub-machine guns.

Conversation

Russian conversation is never trivial. Within minutes, the subject is the meaning of life and philosophical discussion. On the whole, the Russians are happy to talk about anything, but it is a mistake for a foreigner to try and make dirty jokes in mixed company. A pair of saucy knickers, intended as a jokey Christmas present from an English actress to a Russian actress, got a very frosty reception.

Rude words in regular use in mixed company include *svoloch*, used in the same way but not having the same literal meaning as 'bastard' in English; and *zhulik*, meaning a crook. There are lots of other very rude words that would probably only be used between consenting male businessmen when discussing the terms of a deal, telling each other what they would do or require the other to do with each other's sexual organs before agreeing to the terms.

Sexual organs also have a direct bearing on the slang term for a 'big shot' which is *bolshaya shishka* – literally, a big fir cone.

There is also colourful slang for everything to do with money: for instance, money in general can be called *kapusta* (cabbage), a million roubles is called a *limon* (lemon); a billion roubles is an *arbus* (watermelon). A *shtuka* is 1000 roubles, but it is also the ordinary word for a thing. This means that you could find yourself haggling in the market and saying: "A *shtuka* for that *shtuka*? You can't be serious!"

New Russians have rather boorish turns of speech or slang, such as '*kruty*' meaning 'cool' (literally: tight). Whereas in the old Soviet days, the verb used for 'obtain' in Russian was '*dostat*', which carries the flavour of 'managed to get hold of with difficulty', New Russians simply say "*ya vzyal*" – "I took..." When New Russians talk about getting a roof ('*krysha*') over their heads, they are using a slang term for protection against other racketeers.

Language and Ideas

Russian is an expressive, concise and beautiful language. When people talk, a lot of little words which would be used in other languages are left out. For example, a telegram which one intellectual sent to another on the news of the triumph of democracy after the attempted coup in August 1991 read: '*Neuzheli dozhili?*' – 'Is it possible that we have lived to see this day?'

Nouns are masculine, feminine, or neuter, and have cases like Latin or German (nominative, accusative, genitive, etc.). Russian verbs have a twist which adds zing to the language for they enjoy an inscrutable and elusive quality called 'aspect', as well as mood and tense.

But whilst their language is capable of precision, it cannot be denied that the Russians themselves are prolix. They 'go on' a bit. Opening ceremonies, closing ceremonies, movies and novels, all are four times as long as anyone else's.

Russian television is the only such medium in the world where there are genuinely free discussion programmes with no pre-agreed agenda or questions planted in the audience. Not only that, but the television station will stay on the air as long as the discussion goes on. During the early heady days of *glasnost*, people in St. Petersburg and Moscow used to stay up all night watching open-ended discussion programmes until employers and ministries begged for a moratorium so that everyone could get some sleep.

Russian is very inventive and responsive, ready for delicious word-games and foreign borrowings, without any of the defensive vapours of other countries' institutions such as the Académie Française. Russian examinations are taken orally, even in mathematics and other subjects that you would think needed a ruler and a bit of paper.

Whole books have been written on the Russian prefix. For instance: *spal* means slept; *po-spal* means to take a nap; *pro-spal* means overslept; *pere-spal* means slept with, made love to, and *zaspal* means to smother a baby in your sleep.

There has been an explosion of English terms into everyday Russian, partly due to the Russian's passionate embrace of new computer technology. The Russians are world leaders in piracy of software: it is estimated that 90% of the software in use in Russia is illegally copied. A hybrid language called 'Russlish' has emerged in which English vocabulary is used with Russian case-endings, e.g: *'downloadirovat'*.

The Russians love acronyms: *gulag*, for example is a word made up of parts of words meaning the state prison system. *Kolkhoz* is made up of part of the word for collective and part of the word for farm, and in the same way *sovkhoz* is 'council farm' (the word *soviet* is simply the ordinary Russian noun for 'council' both in the sense of a piece of advice and a group of people/local administrators). The Russians gave the world *sputnik* (the Russian for 'traveller'), *cosmonaut* and *intelligentsia*.

There are various concepts conveyable only in Russian, including: *toska* – a yearning, sad feeling; *poshlost* – vulgarity, cheapness – this can be used of ideas as well as people and things; *skuchno* – very frequently used to mean 'we miss you', but also, 'fed up' or even 'tiresome'.

There is a story about an English academic who wrote his doctoral thesis on the subject of the imperative form of the Russian verb. He was flying home, having completed a massively complicated water-tight theory after months of study in Russian libraries, when he noticed that the 'No Smoking' sign in Russian was in a form that blew his whole theory out of the water.

Russian lends itself nicely to wicked parody, double meaning and 'dead-pan' humour. Centuries of censorship have accustomed readers and audiences to look for a hidden meaning in the words or plot.

Every Russian child learns a tribute at school by Ivan Turgenev: 'Ah, mighty, powerful Russian language! How could it be that you were not also given to a great people!'

The Author

Elizabeth Roberts has always regarded Russia as a kind of disease. She caught it herself at the age of 14, and has so far failed to shake it off. In fact, she finds that as she gets older, she suffers more and more frequent bouts of it and has to go there two or three times a year.

She was making quite a good recovery for a while in her 20s and 30s, working as a journalist on various newspapers, but experienced a severe set-back in 1981 when she married John Roberts, then the director of a Foreign Office-funded organization dealing with the Russians.

The combination of frequent Russian visitors to their London home and visits both official and unofficial to what her husband calls 'that country' made any prospect of recovery remote.

The possibility that the infection may be passed by close contact within families is raised by the fact that her elder daughter chose to study Russian at university before escaping onto the stage. Her younger daughter appeared as an opera singer to be immune, until she was caught practising Olga's aria from *Eugene Onegin* in the bath with a perfect Russian accent.

The Roberts now live in a pine forest in Scotland where they have built a *dacha* and filled it with the usual quota of smelly old dogs and ikons in every corner. As one of their closest friends in Moscow says: "It takes all sorts, doesn't it?"